EX LIBRIS

QUEEN'S GATE JUNIOR SCHOOL

The Wayland Book of
Common British Birds
A Photographic Guide

Nick Williams

Front cover pictures (clockwise from top left): Mute Swan; Blue Tit; Black-Headed Gull; Greenfinch; Kestrel; Robin.

Title page picture: A Mute Swan with cygnets.

Contents page pictures (from top): Song Thrush; Jay; Goldfinch; Kestrel.

Editor: Anna Girling
Designer: Loraine Hayes

Picture Acknowledgements
All photographs supplied by Nick Williams except: P. Castell 12 (inset), 22 (bottom), 29 (bottom); T. Mason 39 (bottom left), 40 (top left); I. Olsen 38 (bottom right). Artwork on page 44 supplied by Nick Hawken.

First published in 1992 by
Wayland (Publishers) Ltd
61 Western Road, Hove,
East Sussex BN3 1JD. England

British Library Cataloguing in Publication Data

Williams, Nick
Wayland Book of Common British Birds:
Photographic Guide
I. Title
598.2941

HARDBACK ISBN 0-7502-0533-4

PAPERBACK ISBN 0-7502-0890-2

Typeset by Type Study, Scarborough, England
Printed and bound in Italy by G. Canale and C.S.p.A., Turin.

Contents

Introduction

There are about 8,650 species of birds in the world. Of these, about 500 have been seen at some time in Britain. However, only about 250 of them are seen here regularly by birdwatchers. In fact over 100 have been seen on fewer than ten occasions.

Of the 250 species, I have chosen fifty birds which I consider to be common for this book. All of them can be found without too much trouble. They are birds that can be seen in gardens, school grounds and parks, while out walking or while driving along in a car.

The birds you see will depend to a certain extent on where you live. House Sparrows, Starlings and Blackbirds are part of everyone's daily life, both in towns and the countryside. On the other hand, birds such as Nuthatches and Great Spotted

Woodpeckers are fewer in number. They are more likely to be seen in large gardens, parks and woodlands. By the coast, the Herring Gull will probably be the commonest and noisiest bird. The Oystercatcher may also be a familiar sight in coastal parts of Britain.

Some birds, such as Swallows and House Martins, are only seen in Britain during the summer. These birds eat insects, and they migrate south to Africa in winter to find food.

Below: Spotted Flycatchers migrate to Britain for the summer. They are often seen perching on posts.

Below: Chaffinches are common visitors to gardens.

There are many ways to identify birds. As well as noting their shape, size and colour, their behaviour gives important clues. Also, all birds sing, and it is useful to learn their songs. In the case of the Willow Warbler and the Chiffchaff this may well be the only way of telling the two birds apart!

It is a good idea to keep a birdwatcher's diary or notebook. You will need to note down the species, number, behaviour, eating habits and calls or songs of the birds you see. You could even make quick sketches.

This book is intended for use by teachers and children alike, and also by any beginner birdwatcher.

Above: Beautiful Mute Swans can be found in all parts of Britain – on village ponds, lakes, rivers and estuaries.

Right: Robins sing throughout the year.

Below: Black-Headed Gulls, here in winter plumage, can be seen in towns inland as well as on the coast.

House Sparrow 14.5 cm

The House Sparrow is probably the most familiar to us of all the small birds in Britain. Often thought of as just a little brown bird, the male in fact has a grey head, black bib, brown back streaked with black, and a white bar on its wings. Females and young are a paler mixture of browns, buffs and greys.

House Sparrows like to make their nests in the nooks and crevices of buildings, so they can always be found near human dwellings. They also nest in holes in trees and in nest boxes. Sometimes, they build an untidy domed nest out of dried grass and feathers in bushes or ivy. They normally have three broods in a year.

House Sparrows have finch-like beaks for eating seeds, but they will eat almost anything put out for them on a bird table. During the breeding season, however, their diet consists mainly of insects. They can often be seen in large flocks and they can be a nuisance to gardeners if they decide to attack a vegetable patch or flowerbed.

Above: The male House Sparrow is a more attractive bird than many people think. It has grey, black and brown colouring. Above left: The female is much plainer than the male.

Starling 21.5 cm

Starlings are well known but often unpopular birds. This is because they live in large flocks, both in towns and the countryside, and can make a lot of noise and mess.

A small flock of Starlings can eat up the contents of a well-stocked bird table within a few minutes. Suet and cheese are favourite foods, but they will eat almost anything. Starlings are, in fact, a great friend to the gardener, because they eat thousands of leatherjackets (the larvae of craneflies, or 'daddy-long-legs') and other grubs which eat plants.

Starlings make untidy nests out of straw in holes in buildings or trees. They will also nest in nest boxes if the hole is big enough for them.

Starlings look black from a distance, but in fact their plumage has a beautiful green or purple sheen when the light catches it. They have yellow beaks. In winter their bodies are

covered in white spots. Young birds are grey-brown.

Starlings may look like Blackbirds, but they are smaller and their wings are more pointed. They are normally seen in groups, rather than alone.

Above: A Starling in winter has white tips on its feathers, giving it a spotted appearance.

Starlings are wonderful mimics. They have been known to fool people by accurately imitating the ring of a telephone or doorbell.

Left: Starlings in summer, showing the green sheen to their plumage.

Blackbird 25 cm

Blackbirds belong to the thrush family. The females and young are brown all over, with darker spots on their breasts. The male, however, is black all over, with a yellow-orange beak and a yellow ring round the eyes. Blackbirds are prone to albinism, and there have been many sightings of pure white birds.

Blackbirds usually build nests in bushes and hedgerows. They often nest as early as March and may continue breeding until August, producing up to three clutches. The round, cupped nest is made of grasses held together with mud. The young are fed by their parents almost entirely on worms, but adult birds eat a variety of things, including insects, fruits and berries.

The male Blackbird has a beautiful song, which it sings throughout the breeding season. It also gives out an excited chatter when disturbed.

Above: A male Blackbird has a yellow beak and ring round its eyes.

Left: The female's brown plumage helps to camouflage it from predators when it is nesting.

Robin 14 cm

The Robin, or 'robin redbreast', is an extremely popular bird. It is Britain's national bird. Its eye-catching orange (not red) front extends over the eye and forehead and has a bluish-grey border. Males and females look alike. The young have a dark brown, speckled plumage.

Robins sing a beautiful, sad-sounding song throughout the year. When they are not breeding, the females have their own territory and they, too, sing. Robins are very territorial and become extremely fierce towards other Robins which wander into their 'patch'.

Robins normally start breeding in mid-April. Their nests are always well hidden and are made out of dead leaves, moss and grass, and lined with hair. They will nest in open-fronted nest boxes or old kettles, especially if they are in a quiet spot or in ivy. They have two or three broods in a year.

**Above: The Robin's breast is actually orange, not red.
Below: Robins' nests are usually well hidden.**

Song Thrush 23 cm

The Song Thrush is very similar to the Mistle Thrush (see page 38), except that it is about 3.5 cm shorter. It has a plain brown back and very pale orange breast covered in black spots. When Song Thrushes fly they reveal orange 'arm-pits' underneath their wings.

The Song Thrush is found on the edges of woodlands, in hedgerows and in parks and gardens, where it also nests. It lines its cup-shaped nest with mud and lays blue eggs with black spots on them.

As its name suggests, and like all thrushes, the Song Thrush loves to sing. It will often sing until after dark.

Song Thrushes eat worms, slugs, insects, fruit and berries. They have also developed a remarkable ability to crack open snails. They hold the snail in their beak and smash it against a stone.

Other thrushes include Fieldfares (25.5 cm) and Redwings (21 cm), which migrate to Britain from Scandinavia in winter.

Above: Male and female Song Thrushes look identical.
Inset: Fieldfares are winter visitors to Britain. They also belong to the thrush family.

Wren 9.5 cm

The tiny Wren is one of the most numerous birds in Britain. After a series of mild winters it can out-number all other birds, but its population is seriously cut by bad weather.

The Wren is found in almost every type of habitat – from sea cliffs to moorlands and mountains. It is a secretive bird and will live anywhere it can find cover to hide in. It rarely visits bird tables, even when food is scarce. It can sometimes be tempted with cheese or suet, but normally prefers to search for insect larvae and spiders.

The Wren is more likely to be heard than seen, because it has an incredibly loud voice for such a small bird. When it is seen, its small size and cocked tail make it unmistakable. However, it is not Britain's smallest bird – Goldcrests and Firecrests measure just 9 cm.

Wrens will nest almost anywhere, but particularly like old tree trunks covered in a creeping plant, such as ivy. The male bird makes a number of dome-shaped nests, and the female chooses one she likes.

In very cold weather thirty or forty Wrens may be found roosting together in one nest box, huddled together for warmth. The record is sixty-one in one box.

Below: Wrens can be identified by the way they cock their tails.
Left: Wrens normally build a domed nest. This one used an old Swallow's nest, and the roof of a shed for the top.

Great Tit 14 cm

The Great Tit is the largest member of the tit family. It has a green back, black and white head and black stripe down a yellow breast. The male has a much broader black stripe than the female. The Great Tit is found in woodlands, fields and gardens.

Like all tits, it is a very acrobatic bird. It uses its agility to find food such as insects, insect larvae, spiders, slugs and, in spring, plant buds. Outside the breeding season, Great Tits will eat cheese, suet, sunflower seeds and peanuts from a bird table. Their large size also enables them to crack open acorns and hazelnuts. They hold the nut in their feet and hammer at it with their beak.

Like all tits, Great Tits normally only lay one clutch a year, sometimes containing as many as twelve or thirteen eggs. The eggs hatch in May, when there are plenty of moth caterpillars to feed the young.

Great Tits like to sing and have an incredible range of calls. Fifty-seven different ones have been recorded.

Above: A male Great Tit. The female has a thinner black stripe on her breast.
Inset: Newly-hatched chicks in a nest box.

Blue Tit 11.5 cm

The Blue Tit is the best known of the tit family. It is smaller than the Great Tit and has a distinctive blue crown, wings and tail. Like the Great Tit, it is really a woodland bird which has adapted to live in human environments. The Blue Tit is a popular garden bird and is a frequent user of nest boxes and bird tables.

Blue Tits are both acrobatic and agile, and can often be seen hanging upside-down, either from bird tables or while searching for small green moth caterpillars, on which they feed their young.

Blue Tits lay the first of their eggs (about seven to twelve of them) in early May. The young hatch after about two weeks and are then fed by both parents.

Out of twelve young Blue Tits that may leave the nest only one, on average, will survive to breed the following year. Many are killed by predators.

Above: This young Blue Tit has just grown feathers.

Left: Sunflower seeds and suet are favourite foods of the Blue Tit.

13

Coal Tit 11.5 cm

The Coal Tit's colouring lacks the yellow, blue and green of other tits. It is about the same size as a Blue Tit, and has a black crown, white cheeks, brown back and buff-grey belly. It has a distinctive white patch on the back of its black head.

Unusually, the Coal Tit likes to live among conifer trees. In fact, along with the Goldcrest, it is often the only bird commonly found in conifer forests. It usually nests close to the ground, or even under ground, at the base of a tree. It also likes to nest in old stone walls.

However, the Coal Tit is also a common visitor to garden bird tables and can become almost tame, often showing no fear of humans. It also appears fearless towards larger birds.

Coal Tits take nuts and store them away for when food is scarce. However, they do not always remember where they have put them!

The Coal Tit's diet is similar to that of the Blue Tit and the Great Tit, but also includes large amounts of cone seeds.

Left: Coal Tits have a distinctive white patch on the back of their heads.

Below: Coal Tits like to live among conifer trees.

Dunnock 14.5 cm

The Dunnock is a very common British bird. It is often called the Hedge Sparrow, although it is not related to the sparrow family at all. At first sight it appears to be a brown, sparrow-like bird, but a closer look will reveal a blue-grey head and breast, a chestnut-brown back and wings with dark streaks, orange legs and a thin beak. Males and females look alike.

Dunnocks creep around beneath bushes and hedgerows, looking for insects, spiders and small worms to eat. They are fairly shy, visiting bird tables only when other birds are not around. In fact they normally prefer to pick bits of food up off the ground below the table.

The Dunnock's beautifully-built nest, in which it lays four or five blue eggs, can be found in bushes or hedges from April to June. Dunnocks have two, or sometimes even three, broods each year.

The Dunnock's light, musical song is a common sound throughout the spring and summer months.

Above: Dunnocks can be confused with House Sparrows. Unlike the House Sparrow, the Dunnock has a grey head and breast and a chestnut-brown back.
Inset: Dunnocks build neat nests lined with moss.

Chaffinch 15 cm

Like all British garden birds, the Chaffinch is really a bird of woodland and copses. Chaffinches can be found in a variety of habitats, however, and are among the most abundant of European birds. During the winter they often form large flocks in the open countryside and on the edges of woodland, searching for seeds to eat.

The male is a beautiful bird, with a reddish body and grey head. It is easily recognizable in flight, when it reveals white bars on its wings and white outer tail feathers. The female also has these features, but is mainly pale brown and grey over the rest of the body.

Above: The male Chaffinch is one of the most colourful British birds. Inset: The female Chaffinch is much paler than the male.

Chaffinches start to establish territories early in the year, by repeating their short, trilling song over and over again. They also have a distinctive 'pink-pink' call.

The neat nest is made of grasses, mosses, lichens, spiders' webs, feathers and hair. It is usually built in a bush or in the fork of a tree.

16

Greenfinch 14.5 cm

The male Greenfinch's plumage is a mixture of yellows and greens with dashes of grey. Its forked tail has a dark tip. The female is a duller, slightly browner version of the male and could be confused with a female House Sparrow.

Greenfinches are regular visitors to bird tables. They are fairly aggressive and will fight other birds for food. They eat mainly seeds and are particularly fond of sunflower seeds. They have also discovered how to hang on to peanut holders. This garden food supply is particularly important in late winter and early spring, when natural food can be hard to find.

The male Greenfinch's twittering song is often followed by a wheezing sound. It can be heard as early in the year as January. Greenfinches nest in bushes, hedgerows and, occasionally, trees.

**Above: A male Greenfinch.
Below: The female Greenfinch is duller, but still has yellow patches on its wings.**

Collared Dove 32 cm

Collared Doves eat grain. If they can find enough food and the weather is not too cold, they will breed throughout the year. Normally, however, they have two or three broods a year.

Like most doves and pigeons, they make a flat nest out of twigs and lay two white eggs. Conifer trees are favourite nesting places. Unlike the larger Wood Pigeon, which comes from the same family of birds, Collared Doves like to live in urban areas and often nest close to houses.

Above: A pair of Collared Doves. Inset: Collared Doves often perch on posts and television aerials.

The Collared Dove came from the Balkan area of eastern Europe. The species started to spread westwards in the 1930s, reaching Britain in 1955. It is now widespread, with numbers increasing all the time.

The Collared Dove is a very common sight, often seen perching on telephone wires and television aerials, giving out its monotonous, repetitive 'coo-cooo-coo' call (the middle note being longer than the other two).

Doves and pigeons often pick up grit from the roadside. This helps them to grind up their food.

Wood Pigeon 41 cm

Left: The Wood Pigeon has distinctive white patches on its neck.

The Wood Pigeon is the largest of the pigeons. It is grey, and has two white wing bars which are very noticeable in flight. It also has white patches on the sides of the neck. Its call consists of five notes, unlike the three-note call of the Collared Dove.

Wood Pigeons can sometimes be seen in huge flocks. They can become a serious pest to farmers because they eat crops as well as weeds. Even in towns they can be a nuisance to gardeners, because they like to eat peas, beans and the buds of fruit trees.

In parks and large gardens Wood Pigeons can become quite tame, but in the countryside they are far more wary. If they are disturbed, their wings make a clapping noise as they suddenly take off.

Thousands of Wood Pigeons are shot every year, but this does not seem to affect their numbers. They are still very common.

Below: Feral pigeons are found in most towns and cities.

Wood Pigeons should not be confused with feral pigeons, which live in towns. Feral pigeons are smaller and usually darker in colour.

Great Spotted Woodpecker 23 cm

The Great Spotted Woodpecker is slightly smaller than a Blackbird. It is black and white, with a red patch under the tail. The male also has a small red patch on the back of the head. Young birds have a red head.

Like all woodpeckers, it has two toes facing backwards and two facing forwards. This, along with the stiff tail feathers, allows it to cling on to the trunks of trees. It then drills into the bark with its beak, looking for insects and larvae.

During the breeding season, it sometimes uses its powerful beak to make large holes in nest boxes, so that it can get in and eat the eggs or young of other birds inside. It also feeds on seeds and nuts, especially in winter, and will visit bird tables during cold weather. Like all woodpeckers, it is very agile, and can hang on to bird feeders and bags of nuts.

Great Spotted Woodpeckers drill a new hole in a tree trunk to nest every year.

Green Woodpeckers are also quite common visitors to large gardens, particularly in the south of England.

Above: This male Great Spotted Woodpecker is using its tail to keep its balance. Above left: Young birds have red heads.

20

Pied Wagtail 18 cm

Left: The White Wagtail, common in other parts of Europe, has a paler back than the Pied Wagtail.

The Pied Wagtail can be found anywhere except in woodland and on high mountains. It is often seen in school playgrounds, school fields, industrial areas, farmyards, parks and even city centres. It will visit gardens and will occasionally use bird tables.

Pied Wagtails have an unusual way of walking and running, bobbing their heads up and down and wagging their tails, as they search for insects. They are grey and white birds. The male is darker than the female. They are usually seen alone, but roost together in large groups, especially in winter.

Pied Wagtails nest wherever they can find a sheltered hole – whether in an old shed, modern building or rock face. They will also use open-fronted nest boxes.

Their call is a sharp 'chizzick' sound, which they make while they are flying.

Below: The Pied Wagtail is a common sight in playgrounds and parks in Britain. It is a sub-species of the White Wagtail.

21

Magpie 46 cm

The Magpie is a member of the crow family. It has unmistakable black and white plumage and a long tail. The black feathers have a blue-green and purple sheen when the light catches them.

Magpies can be found in towns as well as in open countryside. They are uncommon in areas where game birds are bred, because in the past many were shot or trapped. However, their numbers are now growing again.

Like all crows, they are intelligent and adaptable. They have a varied diet, which includes the eggs and young of other birds.

Magpies are normally seen alone, but they sometimes gather in noisy, chattering groups, especially when they are not breeding. The Magpie's nest is made of sticks and mud, lined with roots and wool, and has a domed roof.

Above: A Magpie sitting on a school fence. Magpies live in towns as well as the countryside. Left: A young Magpie. The last part of any bird to grow is its tail feathers.

Jackdaw 33 cm

The Jackdaw is the smallest of the four crows commonly seen in Britain. At a distance it appears black all over. However, it has a silvery-grey nape and cheeks and silvery-blue eyes.

Jackdaws normally live in open countryside, where they nest in colonies in holes in trees and cliffs. During the winter they often join Rooks to form large flocks. Sometimes hundreds of birds can be seen in open fields, searching for worms and grubs.

Jackdaws are also seen in towns and cities. They often nest in chimneys of occupied buildings. They will also use churches and cathedrals as nesting and roosting places. Their loud 'jack' call can be heard from far away.

Like Magpies, Jackdaws will take any opportunity to look for food. They can be seen searching for easy pickings from rubbish bins and will also use bird tables.

Above: Jackdaws have steel grey eyes.
Left: Jackdaws are often seen on roofs – and may even nest down a chimney.

Rook and Carrion Crow

From a distance, Rooks and Carrion Crows look very similar. They are about the same size, and appear black all over. The Rook, however, has a grey-white face and throat and a thinner pale bill. As a general rule, Carrion Crows tend to be found alone or in pairs, whereas Rooks are nearly always found in groups.

Rooks always return to the same group nesting sites, called rookeries. These can be hundreds of years old and may contain more than a hundred nests, built high up in tree branches. The Carrion Crow nests alone, in the fork of a tree.

The Carrion Crow, as its name suggests, eats carrion (the flesh of dead animals), as well as worms, insects, plants, scraps from rubbish tips and the eggs of other birds. Rooks take very few eggs and eat far less carrion. They usually eat plants, grubs, insects, larvae and worms.

Scotland has Hooded Crows instead of Carrion Crows.

Above: The Rook has a pale, thinner beak than the Carrion Crow.

Above: The Hooded Crow, seen in Scotland, has a grey body.

Above: The Carrion Crow is completely black, including its beak.

Black-Headed Gull 36 cm

The Black-Headed Gull is the smallest of the British gulls. It is the gull most often found inland and can regularly be seen in fields as they are being ploughed, following the farmer's tractor and feeding on the worms and insect larvae which are suddenly exposed. They can also be seen on playing fields, rubbish dumps and even in gardens, if there is food for them.

Although it looks black from a distance, the adult's head is actually dark chocolate brown during the breeding season (from March to August). In early autumn it loses its dark feathers and these are replaced by white ones, leaving a small dusky spot behind each eye. Its legs and beak are bright red. Young birds have yellowy-orange legs and beaks.

Black-Headed Gulls breed on lakes, rivers, marshland and moorland. Like all gulls, they breed in colonies.

Above: During the breeding season, Black-Headed Gulls have dark brown heads, which look black from a distance. Inset: An adult in winter plumage.

Left: Common Gulls may be mistaken for Black-Headed Gulls in winter.

25

Herring Gull 55–60 cm

Around the coasts of Britain, the Herring Gull is the gull you are most likely to see. In comparison, Lesser Black-Backed Gulls are far less common and have a dark-grey back. Common Gulls (see photograph on page 25) are much smaller and are only 'common' in parts of Scotland.

Herring Gulls nest on cliffs or stretches of dunes. They will also nest among the chimneys of seaside houses and their loud, morning calls can be a nuisance.

They are a common sight in most harbours and many rubbish tips, feeding off anything they can find. They also eat the eggs and young of other birds – even other Herring Gulls. In some areas their numbers need to be controlled, because they hunt and eat the eggs and young of rarer birds, such as Terns. Herring Gulls can also be seen following a tractor as it ploughs farmland near the coast.

Above: The Herring Gull is the commonest gull in Britain.
Inset: In flight, the Herring Gull shows dark wing tips.

Left: The Lesser Black-Backed Gull is much less common than the Herring Gull.

Mute Swan 152 cm

Mute Swans are very large, graceful birds which can be found on village ponds, rivers, large lakes and even coastal waters. They are normally seen in pairs although young birds, and birds that are not breeding, sometimes gather together in large groups.

Mute Swans normally start breeding when they are three years old. If they find a mate to breed with, they usually stay with their mate for life. They build a nest in April, often not bothering to conceal it. This is because they are strong, aggressive birds and can easily defend their nest and territory.

The young, called cygnets, hatch with soft grey down. They are looked after by both the male (called the cob) and the female (the pen). The cygnets may remain with their parents until the next spring, when they will be driven off by the cob.

Swans feed on a variety of water plants. They also graze on grassy banks.

Above: Cygnets with a parent. Cygnets go through an untidy, brown stage. They are sometimes called 'ugly ducklings'.
Inset: Mute Swans have long, strong necks.

Mute Swans are among the heaviest flying birds in the world. One bird, on the River Thames, weighed 25 kg and was too heavy to take off.

Mallard 58 cm

The Mallard is the most common type of duck in Britain. It has adapted well to all kinds of habitats, including those created by humans. Almost every park lake, village pond and stretch of river running through a town or city has Mallards on it.

The male, called the drake, is more colourful than the female, which is brown all over. The female Mallard needs to be camouflaged when sitting on her clutch of up to twelve eggs, which could otherwise be taken and eaten by a fox, stoat or crow. Both male and female birds have a bright purple patch on their wings.

Above: The male Mallard, or drake, has a green head. Inset: This female Mallard is keeping a watchful eye on two ducklings.

The nest is normally on the ground, but Mallards have been known to nest in a wide variety of places – including the window box of a high-rise flat!

Mallards normally feed on water plants, grasses, seeds and insects. Town park ducks, however, will eat almost anything that is offered to them.

28

Moorhen 33 cm

The Moorhen is a familiar waterbird to many people, as it is found on small ponds, lakes, rivers and canals.

Moorhens look almost black from a distance. In fact they have a brown back and wings and grey underparts. They also have a white flash on each side and a white horseshoe-shaped patch under the tail. Their beaks are red with a yellow tip. As they swim, they jerk their heads back and forth.

Moorhens spend a lot of time out of the water, walking or running around searching for food. Their very long toes enable them to walk across lily pads and other floating plants. They eat plants, worms, insects and insect larvae.

They nest on the ground among plants near the water's edge, or among branches overhanging the water. Occasionally they will nest higher up, using the nests of other birds such as Magpies. They have two, or sometimes three, broods a year. The young of the first brood often help their parents to raise the second.

Above: Moorhens have a white patch under the tail. Below: Moorhen chicks may leave the nest for a short time, even within a couple of hours of hatching.

29

Coot 38 cm

Left: Both male and female Coots look like this.

Coots are closely related to Moorhens. Both species belong to the family of birds called rails. Coots generally live on larger patches of water than Moorhens, although the two can often be seen together.

Coots are black all over, with a white beak. They spend more time on the water than Moorhens, and have round lobes on each toe to help them swim more easily.

Nests are larger than those of the Moorhen, but are again built among plants and trees near the water's edge. The young hatch after about three weeks and are able to swim and walk within a few hours of hatching. Young Coots have a bright pink bald head, which may have given rise to the saying 'as bald as a Coot'.

Coots fiercely defend their territory against other Coots during the breeding season. In winter, however, they can form flocks of up to 5,000 birds.

Below: A mother with her newly-hatched chicks, showing their bald heads.

Of British birds, only Coots have pure white beaks.

Canada Goose about 100 cm

Canada Geese were brought to Britain from North America about 300 years ago. People thought they would look attractive on lakes. They quickly spread in the wild.

They are large brown birds with black necks and heads and white cheek patches which extend under their heads. In North America they are migratory birds, but those in Europe usually stay throughout the year.

They can be found on large lakes, but also on rivers in towns and sometimes on quite small stretches of water. They normally live in colonies and prefer to breed on small islands. Canada Geese become very

aggressive if their nests are approached. They make a hissing noise, rather like a swan.

The young, called goslings, are able to fly after about nine weeks, but remain with their parents throughout their first winter. During the winter months Canada Geese come together in flocks.

**Above: Canada Geese are often seen in small flocks.
Left: Another kind of goose is the Greylag Goose. Most farmyard geese are descended from Greylag Geese.**

Grey Heron about 95 cm

Grey Herons are large, grey and white birds with black streaks. They can be seen standing completely still in shallow water, or slowly and deliberately walking along, waiting to snap up fish with their long, dagger-like beaks. As they fly they often give a harsh 'fraank' call.

They feed on fish, frogs, insects, small mammals and, during the breeding season, the young of other water-birds. They can become a pest, particularly in cold weather, when they steal goldfish from garden fish ponds.

Grey Herons are nearly always seen on their own. However, they breed in colonies which can sometimes contain more than 100 nests. The nests, built in trees, are made of sticks and can become quite large.

Eleven weeks after the first egg has been laid the young are ready to leave the nest. Many youngsters die but, if they survive, Grey Herons can live to be twenty years old.

**Above: Grey Herons are always very alert.
Above left: Herons may stand completely still for long periods.**

Pheasant male 76–89 cm, female 53–63 cm

Pheasants were possibly introduced into Britain by the Romans about 2,000 years ago. They have certainly been here since the early eleventh century. Pheasants are game birds and are specially bred to be shot.

The birds introduced into Britain come from a number of sub-species which have interbred over the centuries. In general, the male is a mottled brown and gold, with a dark green face, red eye wattle and very long tail. Some males have a white ring round the neck.

The females are a lighter shade of mottled brown all over and do not have such long tails. This camouflages them when they are sitting on their eggs.

Left: Cock (male) Pheasants have red wattles around their yellow eyes. Below: A cock Pheasant, showing its long tail feathers.

The nest is always well hidden on the ground. A male bird may have a number of mates all sitting on eggs at the same time.

Pheasants are normally seen on the ground, but they roost in trees so that foxes or other animals cannot catch them while they are asleep.

Kestrel 34 cm

Kestrels are the commonest kind of falcon in Britain. They can be seen more often than any other bird of prey. They are found in almost every kind of habitat, except in woods, where the Sparrowhawk (see page 40) predominates.

Kestrels are often seen hunting along the edges of motorways. These edges offer long stretches of undisturbed land, inhabited by the small mammals, insects and birds that Kestrels eat.

Kestrels hunt either by watching and waiting – perched on a telegraph wire, post or branch – or by hovering. The Kestrel can hover for a long time by slightly moving its wings and tail. This enables it to keep its eyes fixed firmly on one spot.

Kestrels will nest in all kinds of places – even in window-boxes on high-rise buildings. They normally nest in holes in trees, old crows' nests, old buildings or on cliff ledges. In some places, open-fronted boxes have been put up specially for Kestrels to nest in.

Other falcons that breed in Britain are the Peregrine Falcon, the Hobby and the Merlin.

Above: A male Kestrel. Males are smaller than females.
Above left: The female Kestrel is much plainer than the male.

Swallow 19 cm

For many people, the arrival of the first Swallows, back from their annual migration, is a sign that summer is coming. British Swallows migrate every winter to southern and central Africa. They fly back again in the spring to breed, the males usually arriving back before the females. The journey in one direction alone can be as long as 8,000 km.

Swallows have a dark blue back, reddish forehead and deeply forked tail. Males have longer tail feathers, called streamers, than females.

They like to nest inside buildings. Farm sheds and garages are often used. The nest is made of mud and grass, lined with feathers, and is often built on a ledge or rafter.

Young Swallows have even shorter streamers than the females and are paler in colouring. At the end of the summer they join the adult birds on their amazing journey back to Africa.

Above: A male Swallow displaying its long streamers. Below: Young Swallows leave the nest when they are a few weeks old.

House Martin 12.5 cm

The House Martin is a close relative of the Swallow, but it appears black, with white under parts and a distinctive white patch on its rump. The forked tail lacks the long streamers of the Swallow. The upper parts are in fact a very dark blue.

Another close relative, the Sand Martin, is slightly smaller and brown and white in colouring. It digs holes in sandy banks to nest in. Both are migratory birds and spend the winter in Africa.

Before humans built houses, House Martins nested on cliffs. Now they are a common sight in towns and cities, as long as the air is not too polluted. Clean air encourages the insects which House Martins feed on.

They build their nests, often in small colonies, on the outsides of buildings under the eaves of roofs. Unlike a Swallow's nest, it is completely enclosed, with just a small entrance hole.

Nests are built of mud and lined with feathers and fine grasses. In dry weather, if there is a lack of mud, nesting may be delayed or not take place at all.

Above: House Martins renovate old nests or, if necessary, build new ones.

Left: A House Martin collecting mud for its nest.

Spotted Flycatcher 14 cm

The Spotted Flycatcher is one of the last migratory birds to arrive in Britain each year. Most return from Africa in early May. It feeds on flying insects, which are not plentiful enough earlier in the year.

It is a fairly plain little bird, with a grey-brown back, pale front and a few streaks (not spots) on the throat and chest. It perches on posts, fences and branches, and then suddenly dashes off in a quick, twisting flight in pursuit of insects. Sometimes, a click can be heard as it snaps shut its beak.

Spotted Flycatchers normally live in open woodland, copses and parks. However, they will also breed very close to houses.

Left: A Spotted Flycatcher waiting to snap up a passing insect.

The nest may be built on a ledge or against a wall or tree, especially if it is covered by ivy or other creeping plant. They may also nest in open-fronted nest boxes.

The Pied Flycatcher also nests in Britain but is far less common. The male is black and white and the female brown and white.

Below: This Spotted Flycatcher raised three young in a hanging basket. You can just see the chicks' heads.

Sixteen other common birds

Mistle Thrush 27 cm Larger than a Song Thrush, the Mistle Thrush has a greyer back and bolder black spots on its throat. It starts singing early in the year and sometimes nests as early as February.

Long-Tailed Tit 14 cm The unmistakable tail of the Long-Tailed Tit is more than half the bird's total length. It is a common bird along woodland edges, but it will also visit bird tables during cold weather.

Tree Sparrow 14 cm Very similar to a House Sparrow, but far less common, the Tree Sparrow can be identified by the reddish-brown cap on its head and its white cheeks with a black spot on them. It is more often seen in countryside than gardens.

Redshank 27 cm Redshanks are wading birds found on marshes, mudflats and meadows near water. They have orange-red legs and beak, and a mottled brown back. When disturbed they make a very loud call of alarm.

Willow Warbler and **Chiffchaff 11 cm**
These two birds are a very similar shape and creamy-brown colour. The Chiffchaff (pictured) usually has darker legs and feet. Their voices are the best way of telling them apart. The Chiffchaff repeats the sound of its name, while the Willow Warbler makes a warble of descending notes.

Goldfinch 12 cm When in flight the golden wing bars, which give the Goldfinch its name, can be seen clearly. Goldfinches are often seen in groups, called 'charms'. They eat seeds from thistles and other plants.

Bullfinch 15 cm The male is a very striking bird, with a deep pink front contrasting with a black and grey head and back. The female is a duller version. Both have a white rump. Bullfinches eat lots of buds and are therefore unpopular with fruit growers.

Nuthatch 14 cm Nuthatches have a plain blue-grey back and black stripe through the eye. They can be found in woods and parks, but will visit bird tables. They are fond of nuts. Nuthatches are good climbers and can walk head first down tree trunks.

Siskin 12 cm Siskins mainly visit Britain in winter. They are a greenish-yellow colour, with bright yellow wing bars. The female is less colourful and does not have the male's black crown. Siskins can become regular visitors to bird tables.

Oystercatcher 43 cm Oystercatchers mainly live near coastal waters, but they can also be found on the banks of rivers and lakes further inland. They use their long, orange bills to find worms, crabs, mussels and cockles. They rarely eat oysters! They have eye-catching black and white wings and make an unusual piping call.

Yellowhammer 17 cm Yellowhammers, with their eye-catching yellow head, can be seen all year round on open ground, in hedgerows and tree plantations. The male is a brighter colour than the female. The sound of the Yellowhammer's song is often written as 'a little bit of bread and no cheese'.

Sparrowhawk 30–38 cm Sparrowhawks are birds of prey that live mainly in woodland, but in cold weather they will visit gardens in the hope of snatching a bird from a bird table. Unlike Kestrels, Sparrowhawks never hover. They fly quickly over hedges and between trees and bushes.

Buzzard about 55 cm   Of the large birds of prey, Buzzards are the commonest in Britain. In some areas they can regularly be seen soaring on their large wings, or sitting on a post. They eat mainly mice, voles and small rabbits.

Tufted Duck 43 cm   This is the commonest duck in Britain after the Mallard. The male (drake) is black and white and the female (duck) dark brown. They dive for food and, provided the water is deep enough, are often seen on park lakes.

Jay 34 cm   The Jay is the most colourful member of the crow family, with a pinkish-brown body and blue and black wings. It is a shy bird and usually gives out a harsh shriek as it disappears into the trees. Jays love acorns and store hundreds of them in readiness for winter.

Great Crested Grebe 48 cm   Once hunted for their plumes (head feathers), which were used to decorate hats, Great Crested Grebes have increased in number and are now a common sight on gravel pits, lakes and canals. In winter they lose their plumes and their colouring becomes less bright.

Attracting birds to your garden

The best way to attract birds into your garden or school grounds is to provide them with food, water, nest boxes and shelter.

Putting out food is most important during cold weather. If you start, however, you must continue until at least the end of the cold spell. This is because birds come to rely on the extra food and may travel some distance to reach it.

The natural supply of seeds, eaten by finches, has often run out by the end of February, so it is a good idea to continue feeding these birds until the end of March.

If you want to feed birds all year round, only put out foods during the breeding season that the birds would find for themselves. These include seeds, meal worms and maggots (available from fishing shops). I have seen a Blackbird trying to feed its young with a beak full of dry white bread, and there have been cases of young birds choking to death as a result of being force-fed the wrong food.

Above: A Blue Tit gets to grips with a hanging feeder filled with peanuts.

Above: A Song Thrush makes a meal of an apple. Try saving windfall fruit to put out in cold weather.

Try to put out as wide a range of foods as possible. Kitchen scraps go down well, particularly potato, cheese, bacon rind, cereals and bread. Always soak bread first, as it may swell in a bird's stomach. Never put out dessicated coconut or salted peanuts.

Collect nuts, berries and windfall fruit in the autumn. You can save them and put them out when there is a cold spell. You can also buy wild bird food, seeds, grains and peanuts from pet shops.

Left: A Great Tit
eats bird cake,
made of suet, from
a coconut shell.

Birds need to replace lost fat in winter. Suet is a useful food and can be put out in grain form. Alternatively, mash it up and put it into the crevices of a tree or a piece of wood hung from a bird table. Suet can also be used to make bird cake. Add nuts and seeds to the melted suet. Pour it into half a coconut shell or margarine tub and allow to set. Hang it upside down outside.

You can grow plants in your garden which will attract birds. Choose plants which produce a lot of nuts, berries and seeds, or which attract insects. Here are some examples: sunflower, cornflower, poppy, holly, elder, rowan, cotoneaster, berberis, honeysuckle and buddleia. Leaving an area of your garden to grow wild is also a good idea. Nettles attract insects; thistles, teasels and chickweed attract finches; brambles offer good nesting places.

Try to put food out in a number of different ways. Bought or home-made bird tables can be hung from a branch of a tree, put on a pole, or even attached to a balcony

Above: Beware of cats! They will attack birds visiting your garden.

or windowsill if you do not have a garden. A bird table with a roof will help to keep the food dry and stop it being covered up by snow in winter.

Hanging feeders are popular with some birds. Others prefer to feed on the ground, but be careful not to encourage this if there are cats around.

Making a nest box

You will need a plank of wood 150 cm long, 15 cm wide and 2 cm thick. Secondhand floor boarding may be used.

Saw the plank into pieces for the back, base, roof, front and two sides, following the measurements on the diagram.

Cut a circle in the front for the entrance hole, 17.5 cm from the bottom. A hole 2.8 cm in diameter will allow Blue Tits, Great Tits and Tree Sparrows to enter but keep out House Sparrows. House Sparrows need a hole 3.8 cm in diameter. Starlings need a larger box and an entrance hole of at least 4.5 cm in diameter.

Make one or two small drainage holes in the base of the box.

Fix the joints with screws or nails. Attach the roof with a hinge (a rubber one provides extra waterproofing) and use hooks and eyes to secure it on either side.

Treat the box with organic exterior wood preservative. Ideally, this should be done two months before the start of the breeding season. You can also use roofing felt to cover the roof and hinge.

Some birds prefer open-fronted boxes. These can be made in the same way, but without the front panel. It helps to extend the base by 3 cm, to make a lip.

Whether you buy a ready-made nest box, or make your own, here are some points to remember:

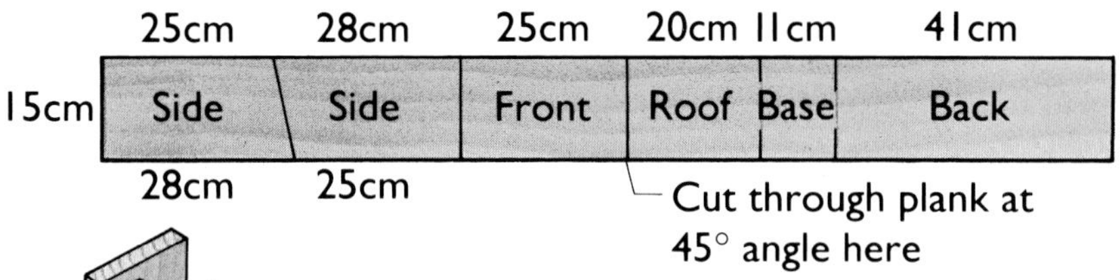

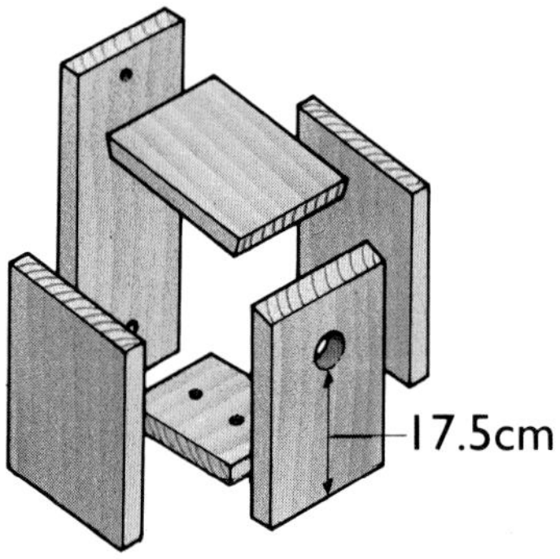

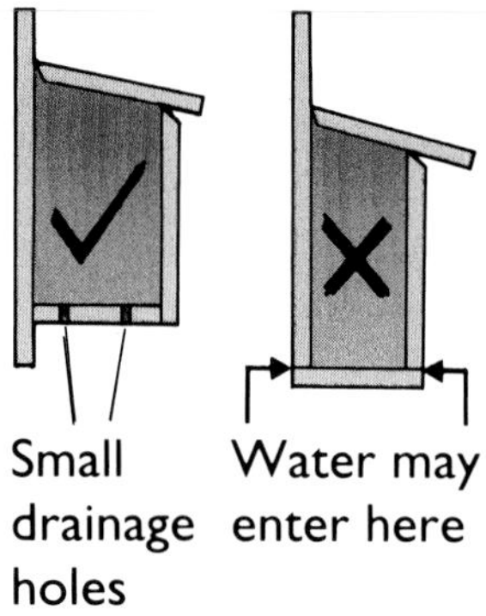

● A new nest box should be put up no later than January or February.
● Make it as difficult as possible for a cat to get at it.
● Make sure the entrance hole does not face south into the sun, or west into the rain.
● Position the box so that the birds have a clear view of the garden from the entrance hole.
● Do not put a perch under the hole. The birds do not need it but a predator may find it useful.
● Make sure you can lift the lid off so that you can clean the box out in the autumn.

The diagram shows the plank measurements:

15cm	Side	Side	Front	Roof	Base	Back

25cm, 28cm, 25cm, 20cm, 11cm, 41cm (top); 28cm, 25cm (bottom, Side)

Cut through plank at 45° angle here

17.5cm

Small drainage holes ✓   Water may enter here ✗

Rubber hinge
Roofing felt
Hook and eye

Children should not attempt to make a nest box without the help of an adult.

44

Bird surveys

Above: Top of the chart – House Sparrows and Starlings at a bird table.

Over the years, many garden bird counts and bird table surveys have been carried out. During January and February, 1991, I surveyed the birds visiting the bird table in my garden. These are my results.

You can carry out your own survey. The birds will vary depending on where you live, but most people will have a similar top 12 – although not necessarily in exactly the same order.

Between 1968 and 1972 the British Trust for Ornithology (BTO) surveyed the number of birds in Britain. Interestingly, the bird that was found to be the commonest – the Wren (10 million pairs) – is not included in my top 12. There could be several reasons for this (see page 11).

The Blackbird was the next commonest bird (7 million pairs), followed by the Chaffinch, Starling and House Sparrow (between 4 and 7 million pairs each). Estimates of the numbers of Robins, Dunnocks and Blue Tits were put at 5 million pairs each.

Glossary

Albinism A lack of normal colouring. An albino bird or animal is completely white.

Bird of prey A bird that hunts and kills other animals for food.

Breeding season The time of year when birds and animals produce their young.

Brood The young that are produced together from one clutch of eggs.

Camouflaged Having feathers or fur of a particular colour to blend in with the scenery. Birds and animals use camouflage to hide from predators.

Clutch A number of eggs laid at one time.

Colonies Groupings of birds that live and grow together.

Conifers Trees, such as pines and firs, that have evergreen leaves and produce cones.

Copse A group of small trees and bushes.

Crops Plants, such as wheat and sugar beet, grown by farmers for food.

Diet The kind of food that a person, bird or animal usually eats.

Down Very soft feathers.

Dunes The ridges of sand that occur on a seashore.

Feral A word used to describe a bird or animal that was once kept and reared by humans but now lives in the wild.

Flocks Groups of birds that feed together.

Game birds Birds that are hunted by humans for sport and for food.

Graze To eat the grass in a field or on a bank.

Habitat The place where a plant or animal naturally lives. Different kinds of habitats suit different plants and animals.

Identify To be able to work out what something is, for example to tell what species a bird belongs to.

Interbred The result of two different but similar types of animals breeding with each other, to produce a cross.

Larvae The young of some animals, particularly insects, that go through a complete change to become adults. Insect larvae often look like slugs.

Lichens Plants that grow on tree trunks and bare ground, usually appearing as a crusty green patch.

Mammal A certain kind of animal which has warm blood and whose young are fed with milk from the mother's body. Mammals are an extremely varied group of animals, ranging from whales to mice. Humans are mammals.

Migrate To travel between two different places every year, so as to spend the summer and winter seasons in different habitats.

Moorland A large area of open land, usually covered in heather, grasses and ferns.

Nape The back of the neck.

Pest An animal that causes a nuisance, often by eating a farmer's crops.

Plumage The feathers of a bird.

Polluted Made dirty. Polluted environments can be harmful to the animals and plants that live in them.

Predators Animals that hunt and kill other animals for food.

Roosting Sleeping or resting on a perch or branch, called a roost.

Species A group of animals or plants that are similar and can breed with each other.

Sub-species A small group of animals or plants from within one species. They share particular characteristics not found in other members of the species.

Territory An area of land which an animal, or pair of animals, claims as its own, usually for breeding. It will defend its territory against other animals.

Wattle A loose fold of skin hanging from a bird's head or throat.

Books to read

Burnie, David *Bird* (Eyewitness Guides)
(Dorling Kindersley, 1988)
Flegg, J. *Birds of the British Isles* (Orbis,
1984)
Holden and Sharrock *The RSPB Book of
British Birds* (Macmillan, 1982)
Wood, Nigel *Birds in your Garden*
(Hamlyn, 1985)

Other resources
Birdwatching Magazine is available monthly
at most large newsagents.
A cassette of bird songs, 'Garden Birds' by
Jean C. Roché, is available from the Bird
and Wildlife Bookshop, 2–4 Princes
Arcade, Piccadilly, London SW17 6DS.

Birdwatcher's code

1 The birds always come first. Never
disturb or frighten them. Try to keep
away from their nests. Remember: it
is against the law to take birds' eggs.
2 All types of habitat must be
preserved. Make sure you never
damage habitats in any way, for
example by dropping litter or pulling
up plants.
3 Always ask permission before
going on to private land. Do not walk
on crops or leave gates open.

Index

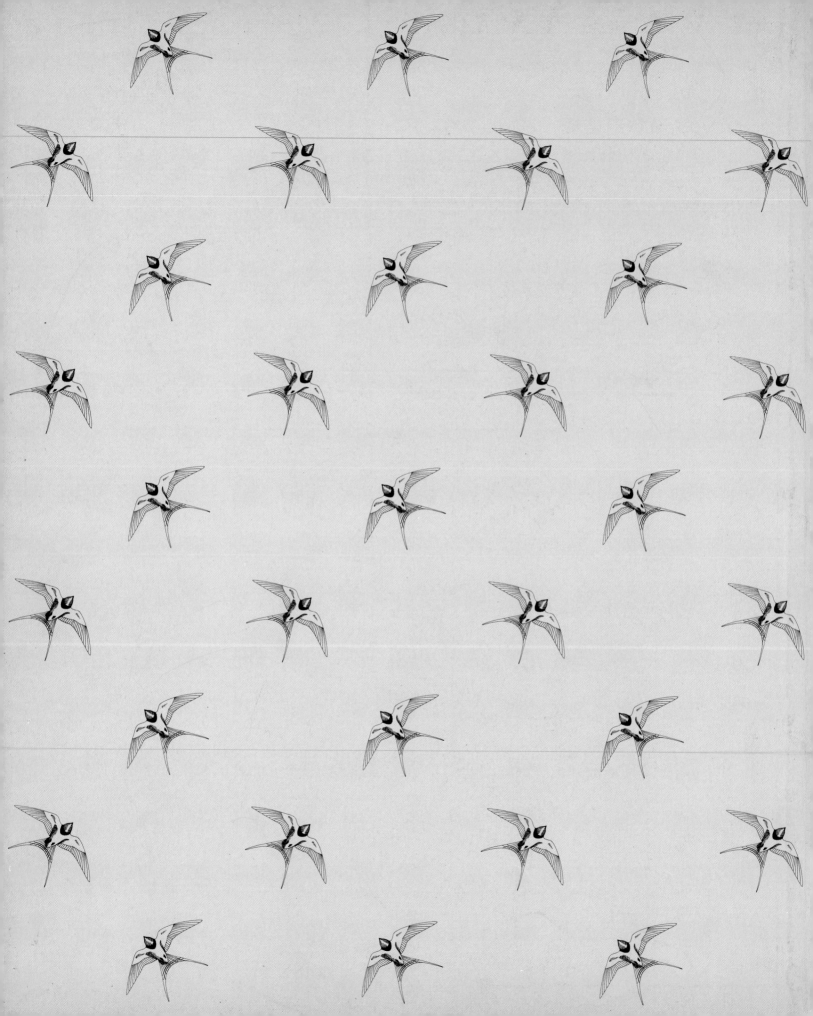